MW00764017

Nativity PTA
Property of
Nativity School

MATH IN OUR WORLD

MEASURING

AT THE POND

By Linda Bussell

Reading consultant: Susan Nations, M.Ed.,
author/literacy coach/consultant in literacy development
Math consultant: Rhea Stewart, M.A., mathematics content specialist

WEEKLY READER®
PUBLISHING

Please visit our web site at www.garethstevens.com
For a free color catalog describing our list of high-quality books,
call 1-800-542-2595 (USA) or 1-800-387-3178 (Canada). Our fax: 1-877-542-2596

Library of Congress Cataloging-in-Publication Data
Bussell, Linda.
      Measuring at the pond / by Linda Bussell.
         p. cm. — (Math in our world level 3)
      Includes bibliographical references and index.
      ISBN-10: 0-8368-9291-7 — ISBN-13: 978-0-8368-9291-8 (lib. bdg.)
      ISBN-10: 0-8368-9390-5 — ISBN-13: 978-0-8368-9390-8 (softcover)
        1. Metric system—Juvenile literature. 2. Pond ecology—Juvenile literature.
    3. Insects—Juvenile literature. I. Title.
    QC92.5.B87 2009
    530.8'12—dc22   2008010956

This edition first published in 2009 by
Weekly Reader® Books
An Imprint of Gareth Stevens Publishing
1 Reader's Digest Road
Pleasantville, NY 10570-7000 USA

Copyright © 2009 by Gareth Stevens, Inc.

Creative Director: Lisa Donovan
Designer: Amelia Favazza, *Studio Montage*
Copy Editor: Susan Labella
Photo Researcher: Kim Babbitt

Photo Credits: cover, title page: James Randklev/Getty Images; p. 4: Photodisc; pp. 6, 8, 10: Hemera
Technologies; pp. 7, 13: S&P&K Maslowski/FLPA; pp. 9, 10, 11, 13, 17, 18, 19: Totallybuggin.com;
p. 16: Corbis; p. 21: USDA

All rights reserved. No part of this book may be reproduced, stored in a retrieval system, or
transmitted in any form or by any means, electronic, mechanical, photocopying, recording,
or otherwise, without the prior written permission of the copyright holder.

Printed in the United States

1 2 3 4 5 6 7 8 9 10 09 08

Table of Contents

Words that appear in the glossary are printed in **boldface** type the first time they occur in the text.

Chapter 1

A Field Trip

The classroom buzzes with news. The students in Miss Tosh's class are going on a field trip!

Miss Tosh says they will visit the local pond and the area around it. The students will look for different plants and **insects** that live at the pond.

They will pretend they are scientists and observe the insects in their **habitats**. The habitats include the pond, the soil, milkweed plants, other wildflowers, and nearby trees.

They will use their science journals to record what they see, and then they will write reports about their findings to share with the class.

The students will record what they see at the pond for their reports.

Miss Tosh holds up her field guide for the class to see. "This field guide is a book about insects that live near the pond," she says. She opens the book and shows the class what it looks like inside.

"It has pictures and information about the insects and their habitats. The field guide includes measurements. It shows the size of many insects in **centimeters (cm)**. It has information about the plants in the area, too."

Miss Tosh says students will work in pairs to find and identify the insects. Each pair will use a field guide.

Students will use field guides to learn about the insects they see on their field trip.

Field Guide

Hickory Horned Devil
About 10 cm long

Chapter 2

At the Pond

Today is the field trip. The students brought their science journals to record what they see.

Miss Tosh has field guides as well as crayons so the students can draw pictures of insects they spot.

Miss Tosh says the students will look for colors and markings to help them identify the insects. Markings are patterns of color on an animal.

They will estimate the sizes of the insects. They will compare the estimates with the sizes in the field guide.

The bus arrives at the pond. Students put on gloves before starting their investigations.

Milkweed and other wildflowers grow near the pond. They also grow in the field around the pond. These plants are an important habitat for some insects. Their poisonous sap is a source of food for insects such as the monarch caterpillar. The poisonous sap does not harm the monarch caterpillar.

This milkweed is about 90 cm tall. That is longer than a baseball bat!

The students notice many orange and black butterflies flying around the milkweed.

At first all the butterflies look the same. A few are different, though. Adam and Rachel use their field guide to discover that there are two kinds of orange and black butterflies.

Milkweed is a source of food for many different insects.

One of the butterflies is called the monarch, and the other is called the viceroy. Adam notices that the hind wings of the butterflies are different. The viceroy has a black band there, but the monarch does not.

They check the field guide. It says that wingspan is the distance across the widest part of the wings when they are fully open.

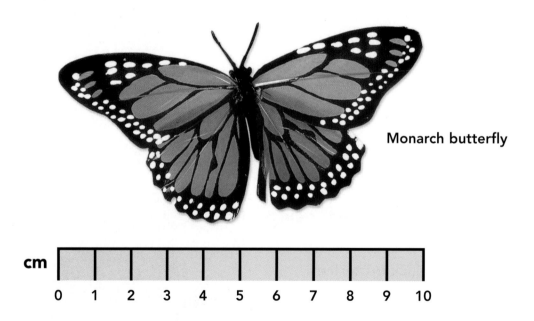

Monarch butterfly

cm

0 1 2 3 4 5 6 7 8 9 10

The monarch's wingspan is about 10 cm, and the viceroy's wingspan is about 8 cm. Rachel records the two butterflies and their wingspans in the journal. Then Rachel sees something green hanging from a milkweed stem.

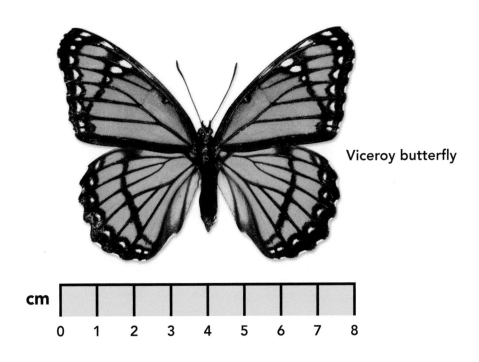

Viceroy butterfly

cm
0 1 2 3 4 5 6 7 8

Adam finds a picture of the object in the field guide and learns that it is a monarch **chrysalis**, or pupa. The monarch caterpillar turns into a chrysalis before it becomes an adult butterfly. It remains in the chrysalis for 10–12 days.

The process of changing from a caterpillar to a pupa to a butterfly is called metamorphosis. The chrysalis in the field guide measures more than 2 cm in length. Rachel estimates this chrysalis is almost the same size as the one in the field guide.

She notes this in their journal. She draws a picture of the chrysalis.

A monarch butterfly chrysalis, or pupa, is shown in different stages of development.

Daisy and Ruben are also exploring the milkweed. They see yellow, black, and white caterpillars of different sizes. Adam reads in the field guide that they are all monarch caterpillars that will grow into monarch butterflies.

Caterpillars grow in stages called instars. Between instars, the caterpillars shed their skin to keep growing. There are five instars in all.

13

Daisy and Ruben find a table in their field guide that compares the sizes of monarch instars.

Daisy and Ruben compare the caterpillars they see with the information in the table. They record their observations in their journal.

Monarch Butterfly Instars

Stage	Approximate Length
First Instar	About $\frac{1}{2}$ cm
Second Instar	Almost 1 cm
Third Instar	About 1 cm to $1\frac{1}{2}$ cm
Fourth Instar	About $1\frac{1}{2}$ cm to $2\frac{1}{2}$ cm
Fifth Instar	About $2\frac{1}{2}$ cm to $4\frac{1}{2}$ cm

Chapter 3

Antlions, Luna Moths, and Hickory Horns

Kami sees several small, circular pits in the sandy soil around the pond. She wonders what they could be.

Sydney finds a picture of the pits in the field guide. They read that antlion larvae build these pits to catch prey. The antlion larva in the field guide measures less than 1 cm.

The adult antlion is much larger than the larva. The adult in the field guide has a wingspan of almost 1 dm. One **decimeter (dm)** equals 10 centimeters.

Kami records information about the antlion larva in their journal.

Some antlion larvae are smaller than 1 cm. Adult antlions can have wingspans up to 1 dm.

dm

0   1

cm

0   1

Hickory trees near the pond are another insect habitat. This type of tree can grow to be 40 m tall. One **meter (m)** equals 100 centimeters. Forty meters is longer than three school buses parked end to end.

Sydney spots a large, green moth on a tree trunk. It is an adult luna moth. This is a lucky find because luna moths are an endangered species in some areas.

This luna moth is sitting high in the tree, more than a meter above their heads. The field guide says that some adult luna moths have a wingspan of more than 11 cm.

Adult luna moths can have wingspans of more than 11 cm.

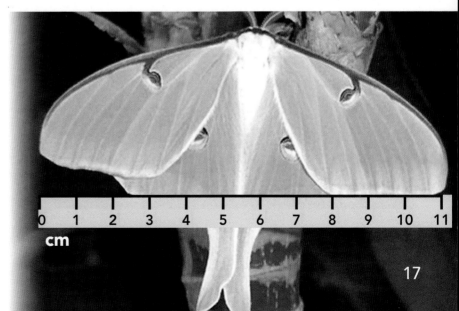

Benjamin and Carl also are looking among the hickory trees for insects. They are trying to find a caterpillar called the hickory horned devil. It is fierce-looking, but harmless to people.

They find several hickory horned devil caterpillars in the twigs of a hickory tree. The caterpillars are eating hickory leaves. The caterpillars are different sizes and have orange and black spines behind their heads.

Carl reads the field guide. It shows a hickory horned devil that is about 10 cm long. Benjamin records the information in their science journal. Then he draws a picture of this insect.

The hickory horned devil caterpillar is harmless to people.

Carl reads in the field guide that the hickory horned devil is the caterpillar stage of the adult regal moth. Like the hickory horned devil, the regal moth can grow very large. Regal moths have a wingspan of up to 10 cm long.

Carl and Benjamin look around, but they do not find any regal moths. This is probably because regal moths are nocturnal, or active at night.

Then the boys hear Miss Tosh call the class together. Miss Tosh collects the crayons, markers, and field guides. She collects their gloves. The students climb on board the bus.

Regal moth

cm

Chapter 4

Going Home

The students settle on the bus. They are excited about their day and talk all at once about the different insects they saw at the pond.

Miss Tosh asks them to name some of the insects they saw. The students talk about some of the surprising things they learned.

"We saw lots of monarch butterflies," says Rachel. "We read that some monarch butterflies fly more than 4,000 **kilometers (km)**!"

"Correct," says Miss Tosh. "Some monarchs migrate from southern Canada, across the United States, to central Mexico. That is a very long trip for such a small insect!"

The students saw many insects at the pond.

Miss Tosh asks her students to share some of their drawings. The students show the pictures they made.

They show drawings of butterflies, dragonflies, mantids, caterpillars, and even a giant water bug. The students also discuss the journal entries they made at the pond.

"You have learned a lot today," says Miss Tosh. "I am proud of you. I cannot wait to read your reports."

It has been a busy day. This has been a fun field trip. The bus driver starts the bus, and they head back to school. The class will always remember this trip.

What Did You Learn?

1. A hickory tree can be 40 m high. A hickory horned devil is about 10 cm long. How many hickory horned devils could you fit into the height of a hickory tree?

2. An antlion larva measures less than 1 cm. Think about what else might measure less than 1 cm.

Use a separate piece of paper.

Glossary

centimeter (cm): a metric unit that is used to measure length or distance. 100 centimeters = 1 meter

chrysalis: the pupa of a butterfly

decimeter (dm): a metric unit that is used to measure length or distance. 1 decimeter = 10 centimeters

habitat: the place or environment where a plant or an animal naturally lives and grows

insect: class of small animals. Insects have six legs and three main body parts called the head, thorax, and abdomen. Many insects have one or two pairs of wings.

kilometer (km): a metric unit that is used to measure length or distance. 1 kilometer = 1,000 meters

meter (m): a metric unit that is used to measure length or distance. 1 meter = 100 centimeters

Index

About the Author

Linda Bussell has written and designed books, supplemental learning materials, educational games, and software programs for children and young adults. She lives with her family in San Diego, California.